REAL WORLD MATH: PERSONAL FINANCE

SAVING FOR THE FUTURE

STUDENT LOAN

CECILIA MINDEN

Published in the United States of America by Cherry Lake Publishing
Ann Arbor, Michigan
www.cherrylakepublishing.com

Math Education: Dr. Timothy Whiteford, Associate Professor of Education at St. Michael's College
Financial Adviser: Kenneth Klooster, financial adviser at Edward Jones Investments
Reading Adviser: Marla Conn, ReadAbility, Inc.

Photo Credits: © realinemedia/Deposit Photos, cover, 1, 29; © R. MACKAY PHOTOGRAPHY, LLC/Shutterstock Images, 5; © Twin Design/Shutterstock Images, 7; © Vinnstock | Dreamstime.com - Budgeting, Savings And Money Planning Photo, 9; © Monkey Business Images/Shutterstock Images, 10, 23; © Deerfield Photo/Shutterstock Images, 13; © Photodisc/Thinkstock Images, 15; © Pinkcandy/Shutterstock Images, 17; © bennyartist/Deposit Photos, 19; © Lisa F. Young/Shutterstock Images, 21; © arek_malang/Shutterstock Images, 25; © gkrphoto/Thinkstock Images, 26; © Arina P Habich/Shutterstock Images, 27

Library of Congress Cataloging-in-Publication Data

Minden, Cecilia.
    Saving for the future / Cecilia Minden.
    pages cm. — (Real world math: personal finance)
    Includes bibliographical references and index.
    ISBN 978-1-63362-574-7 (hardcover) — ISBN 978-1-63362-754-3 (pdf) — ISBN 978-1-63362-664-5 (pbk.) —
ISBN 978-1-63362-844-1 (ebook)
    1. Finance, Personal—Juvenile literature. 2. Saving and investment—Juvenile literature. 3. Budgets, Personal—
Juvenile literature. 4. Mathematics—Juvenile literature. I. Title.

HG179.M5256 2016
332.024—dc23   2015008954

Cherry Lake Publishing would like to acknowledge the work of
the Partnership for 21st Century Skills. Please visit www.p21.org
for more information.

Printed in the United States of America
Corporate Graphics

ABOUT THE AUTHOR

Cecilia Minden, PhD, is a literacy consultant and the author of many books for children. She is the former director of the Language and Literacy Program at Harvard Graduate School of Education in Cambridge, Massachusetts. Dr. Minden has always had a savings account. It has helped her reach many of her lifetime goals.

TABLE OF CONTENTS

CHAPTER 1

Why Save Money?

What if today you found a $20 bill on the sidewalk? Would you put the entire amount in your savings account? Would you spend the $20 as fast as you could? Or would you put some in savings and spend the rest?

Of course, the best choice would be 1 or 3, but 2 might be the most fun! Will "most fun" help you reach financial goals? Not usually. Reaching goals is one reason to save money. A savings account can also help you with unexpected **expenses** and give you security knowing you have your own money to spend.

How much money do you save each week?

There are two kinds of goals: short-term and long-term. For example, you want to take your dad to a movie for his birthday. His birthday is in three weeks. You have three weeks to save enough money to pay for movie tickets and snacks. This is a short-term goal. You are saving the money you need within a short time.

Long-term goals are more expensive items. You need more time to save more money. Maybe you are already saving to pay for college classes or your first car. These are long-term goals.

LIFE AND CAREER SKILLS

Are you saving as much as you can right now? When you see something you would like to buy, always ask yourself, "Do I *need* it, or do I *want* it?" When you satisfy a need, you complete a goal. When you satisfy a want, you fulfill a temporary urge. It is hard to make choices, but you have to, in order to save money.

Saving up to buy the latest cell phone might be a long-term goal depending on the cost.

CHAPTER 2

STRATEGIES FOR SAVING

Saving money takes a little effort and planning. You have to decide to do it. There are some simple strategies you can use to help yourself save money.

First, decide how much you want to save. Make a list of your weekly expenses. Look at the list, and choose what you *need* and what you *want*. This will help you figure out just how much you can set aside for savings. Try to come up with a percentage rather than a dollar amount. That way, if you get some extra money one week, you'll save even more.

Put money in your savings account *first*. Don't skip a week and tell yourself you'll do it next week. Also, put your money someplace where you can't get to it easily. If you don't have a bank account, then put your money in a

Regularly adding money to a savings account is one of the best things you can do for yourself.

Doing extra chores is one way you can earn cash.

closet, in a special box, or in a jar on the top shelf. This will give you time to think about taking money out of your savings. Just remember where you hid your money!

How can you hold on to the rest of your **allowance**? Planning ahead can help to keep you from spending it. Don't carry cash with you unless you are on your way to purchase something you need. Bringing a snack from home can keep you from spending your money on junk food at the mall.

Did you find a great baseball cap that you really want?

Rather than buying it right away, wait a day. Most retail stores will hold an item for you for 24 hours. This gives you time to decide whether you need it or just want it. If you still want to buy the cap, then you need to come up with a plan for how you will pay for it without dipping into your savings. Can you earn extra money babysitting or doing yard work? Can you split the cost with a sibling and then share the cap? Be creative and do the math!

REAL WORLD MATH CHALLENGE

Hannah decides to save 15 percent of her weekly total. Last week, she received a gift of $30.00 for her birthday, $6.00 for her allowance, and $9.00 for cleaning up her neighbor's yard.

- How much money did Hannah take in that week?
- How much did she put into savings?
- How much would she put into savings if she were saving 25 percent of her money?

(Turn to page 30 for the answers)

CHAPTER 3

Do the Math: How Long Will It Take?

Saving for a goal takes patience. As you're waiting for your savings to grow, try to stay positive. Remind yourself that each day you are closer to your goal than you were yesterday or last week or last year. If you don't keep your goal in mind, you're more likely to spend money that you wanted to save.

When making a short-term or a long-term goal, it's important to figure out how long it will take to achieve it. Knowing how long it will take will help you focus on the goal.

How long do you think it would take you to save enough money to buy a new pair of gym shoes?

REAL WORLD MATH CHALLENGE

Jake wants to buy new headphones that cost $79.00 plus 7 percent sales tax. Jake's grandparents gave him $50.00 for his birthday. His allowance is $8.00 a week. He is saving $4.00 a week from his allowance.

- What is the total cost of the headphones?
- How long will it take for Jake to save enough money to buy the headphones?

(Turn to page 30 for the answers)

A calendar can help you stay on track for reaching your goals. Glue a picture of what you want to buy on the date you want to buy it. You could paper clip an envelope to the calendar. Keep your money in the envelope. Then, if you are tempted to use that money on something else, you will be reminded of your goal.

With long-term goals, you have time to seek out more ways to make and save money. A good way to increase your buying power is to open a savings account. The bank will pay you for letting them keep your money.

Opening a savings account is a good way to keep track of how much money you have put aside.

The money you earn is called **interest**. When your money is earning interest, your money makes money for you.

Let's say you have $100.00 and want to open a savings account. You put your money in an account earning 5 percent interest. At the end of one year, you will have $105.00—your original $100.00 plus $5.00 in interest. At the end of two years, you will have $110.25. That's the $105.00 plus $5.25 in interest. Why did you get more interest the second year? Because you earned interest on the interest you made the first year! With interest, not only does your money make money, but the amount of money it makes increases each year.

21ST CENTURY CONTENT

Many banks offer special savings accounts for students who are under 18 years old. They also may offer special interest rates, bank tours, and informative monthly newsletters.

Buying your first car is a good long-term goal.

REAL WORLD MATH CHALLENGE

Tim has just turned 11 years old. He wants to save money so he can buy a used car when he is 16. He gets a weekly allowance of $7.00. When he is 12, he will get $9.00 a week. When he is 14, he will get $12.00 a week. He plans to save 50 percent of his allowance each week.

• How much money will he have in 5 years?

Five years later, Tim turns 16. He decides to wait and buy a car when he goes to college at age 18. Now he **invests** all the money he saved for the car and is earning 10 percent interest.

• How much will he have at age 18?

(Turn to page 30 for the answers)

CHAPTER 4

Do the Math: How Can I Save More?

Do you know where your money goes? To find out, try an experiment. For two weeks, keep a money diary. Write down everything that you buy—from chewing gum to a CD—and the cost of each item. At the end of the two weeks, divide your expenses into these categories: food, clothing, school, and other. Are there a lot of items listed under "other"? Were these items things that you wanted or needed? Circle the items that you could have done without and total up the cost. All that money could have gone to your savings account!

Do you have a smartphone? There are many apps available
to help you keep track of how you spend your money.

REAL WORLD MATH CHALLENGE

Jake's sister Amy also wants to buy the headphones that cost $79.00 plus 7 percent tax. Amy has $25.00 saved already. She wants to buy her headphones in one month (4 weeks). Amy is now saving $4.50 a week from her allowance. She asked her neighbors if she could babysit for them for $3.00 an hour. Mrs. Dillon hired her for 3 hours a week for 2 weeks. Mrs. Nichols hired her for 2 hours a week for 4 weeks.

- Will Amy have enough money to buy the headphones at the end of 4 weeks?

(Turn to page 30 for the answers)

Your money diary will give you a better idea of where to cut expenses. It is easy to spend extra money when you are eating away from home. Bring snacks from home instead. You can also cut expenses by shopping when there are sales and by using **coupons**. Put the money you save into your savings account.

What if you've cut expenses but still need more money to reach your goals? Then you need to find ways to earn extra money. Start by offering to do extra chores around the house. Think about your regular chores. Do you feed the family dog? You could also brush, wash, and walk the dog. First, decide on a fair price for each extra task. Next you'll need to present your list and the prices to your parents. **Negotiate** a price that you all agree is fair.

Ask your parents if you can earn money by doing extra chores.

You might also want to take your job list to your neighbors. Offer to do the same jobs for them. Maybe they will have other jobs they want you to do. Keep a professional attitude. Show up on time, be polite, clean up afterward, and thank them for the work. If you make a good impression, they will hire you again.

LIFE AND CAREER SKILLS

Small savings can really add up. Let's say you spend $12.00 a week on snacks and fast food. What if you put that $12.00 a week in an account earning 5 percent interest instead? At the end of just five years, you will save more than $3,500.00!

It's usually cheaper to bring a bag lunch than to buy from the cafeteria every day.

CHAPTER 5

PLANNING FOR THE FUTURE

Most people have both short-term goals and long-term goals. You want to buy the latest book about your favorite action hero. That's a short-term goal. There is also an awesome guitar you want. That's a long-term goal.

How do you reach both goals? The best way to do this is to create a savings plan. Decide how much to save each week and do the math to divide that savings up. Split the amount you save into long-term goals and short-term goals.

Take advantage of everything offered free at your local library.

Keep track of the money you save and spend. These are skills that will help you for the rest of your life.

21st CENTURY CONTENT

Not everyone has the money to pay for basic needs such as food, clothing, and shelter. Charities collect donations to help care for people in need, both close to home and around the world. Include donations in your budget. Your money will be put to good use.

You are more likely to meet your goals when you keep track of your progress. You need to set up a plan that works for you. Whether your plan is on paper, a calendar, or the computer, the important thing is that you have a plan and you use it.

When you go shopping, check the prices carefully.

You'll be well on your way to figuring out what is best for you when you keep track of how you save and spend your money. It's fun to dream about what you want, but it takes practice to make good decisions about the right things to buy. With a little planning and research, your money can go a long way. Instead of being broke, you'll buy things that you care about. Your money will be working for you.

REAL WORLD MATH CHALLENGE

Mateo has an allowance of $8.00 a week. He decides to create a savings plan. He will give 15 percent of his money to **charity**. Mateo will save 20 percent for long-term goals and 30 percent for short-term goals. The remaining 35 percent is his to spend as he wants.

- How much money goes into each category each week?

(Turn to page 30 for the answers)

College classes are expensive, so it's good to start saving early.

REAL WORLD MATH CHALLENGE ANSWERS

CHAPTER TWO
Page 11
Hannah received $45.00 in one week.
$30.00 + $6.00 + $9.00 = $45.00

If Hannah saves 15 percent, she will put $6.75 into savings. If she saves 25 percent, she will put $11.25 into savings.
$45.00 x 0.15 = $6.75
$45.00 x 0.25 = $11.25

CHAPTER THREE
Page 14
The tax on the headphones is $5.53. The total cost of the headphones, including tax, is $84.53.
$79.00 x 0.07 = $5.53
$79.00 + $5.53 = $84.53

After his birthday, Jake still needs $34.53.
$84.53 − $50.00 = $34.53
He can save $34.53 in 9 weeks.
$34.53 ÷ $4.00 = 9 weeks (8.6 rounded up to 9)

Page 17
By saving 50 percent of his allowance each week, Tim will save $182.00 at age 11.
50% of $7.00 = 0.50 x $7.00 = $3.50
$3.50 x 52 (weeks in a year) = $182.00
Tim will save a total of $468.00 at ages 12 and 13.
50% of $9.00 = 0.50 x $9.00 = $4.50
$4.50 x 52 x 2 (years) = $468.00
Tim will save a total of $624.00 at ages 14 and 15.
50% of $12.00 = 0.50 x $12.00 = $6.00
$6.00 x 52 x 2 (years) = $624.00
After 5 years, on his 16th birthday, Tim has $1,274.00.
$182.00 + $468.00 + $624.00 = $1,274.00

At age 17, Tim has $1,401.40.
10% of $1,274.00 = 0.10 x $1,274.00 = $127.40
$1,274.00 + $127.40 = $1,401.40
Tim's total savings at age 18 is $1,541.54.
10% of $1,401.40 = 0.10 x $1,401.40 = $140.14
$1,401.40 + $140.14 = $1,541.54

CHAPTER FOUR
Page 20
The total cost of the headphones is $84.53.
7% of $79.00 = 0.07 x $79.00 = $5.53
$79.00 + $5.53 = $84.53
Amy needs to save $59.53 more to buy the headphones.
$84.53 − $25.00 = $59.53
In 4 weeks, Amy will save $18.00 from her allowance.
$4.50 x 4 = $18.00
Amy will earn $18.00 babysitting for Mrs. Dillon and $24.00 babysitting for Mrs. Nichols.
$3.00 x 3 hours x 2 weeks = $18.00
$3.00 x 2 hours x 4 weeks = $24.00
Yes, Amy will be able to buy the headphones after 4 weeks.
$18.00 + $18.00 + $24.00 = $60.00

CHAPTER FIVE
Page 28
Each week, Mateo will give $1.20 to charity. He will save $1.60 for long-term goals and $2.40 for short-term goals. He has $2.80 to spend as he wants.
15% = $8.00 x 0.15 = $1.20
20% = $8.00 x 0.20 = $1.60
30% = $8.00 x 0.30 = $2.40
35% = $8.00 x 0.35 = $2.80

Find Out More

BOOKS

Harman, Hollis Page. *Money Sense for Kids.* Hauppauge, NY: Barron's, 2004.

Heckman, Philip. *Saving Money.* Minneapolis: Lerner, 2006.

Holyoke, Nancy. *A Smart Girl's Guide: Money: How to Make It, Save It, and Spend It.* Middleton, WI: American Girl, 2006.

WEB SITES

Hands on Banking
www.handsonbanking.org
Check out an interactive program that teaches banking and money management skills.

Kids.gov: Money
http://kids.usa.gov/money/index.shtml
Learn fun facts, watch games, and play videos related to money at this government site.

PBS: It's My Life—Money
http://pbskids.org/itsmylife/money/managing/article7.html
Read about managing money and other money topics and play some games.

GLOSSARY

allowance (uh-LOU-uhns) money given to someone regularly, especially from parents to a child

charity (CHEHR-uh-tee) an organization that helps the needy, or a gift to such an organization

coupons (KOO-ponz) pieces of paper that give you discounts on purchases

expenses (ik-SPENS-ez) money for a particular job or task

interest (IN-trist) the amount earned on money kept in a bank

invests (in-VESTZ) gives or lends money to something, such as a company, with the intention of getting more money back later

negotiate (nih-GO-shee-ate) to talk over something with others and reach an agreement

INDEX